FOOD

POULTRY

Jillian Powell

HODDER
Wayland

an imprint of Hodder Children's Books

Titles in the series

BREAD   EGGS   FISH   FRUIT
MILK   PASTA   POTATOES
POULTRY   RICE   VEGETABLES

First published in Great Britain in 1997 by Wayland (Publishers) Ltd
Reprinted in 2001 by Hodder Wayland, an imprint of Hodder
Children's Books

Hodder Children's Books,
A division of Hodder Headline Ltd
338 Euston Road
London NW1 3BH

Series Editor: Sarah Doughty
Editor: Liz Harman
Design: Jean Wheeler
Illustration: Peter Bull
Cover: Zul Mukhida – assistant photostylist Bridget Tily

British Library Cataloguing in Publication Data

Powell, Jillian
Poultry. - (Food)
1. Poultry as food – Juvenile literature 2. Cookery (Poultry) –
Juvenile literature
I. Title
641.3'65

ISBN 0 7502 3446 6

Typeset by Jean Wheeler

Printed and bound in Italy by L.E.G.O. S.p.A., Vicenza

Picture acknowledgements

Cephas 4 (top), 8 (top), 11, 13 (bottom), 16 (top), 17 (bottom), 19 (bottom), 20,
21 (both), 22 (top), 23, 25; Chapel Studios 6, 10 (bottom), 18, 19 (top),
22 (bottom); James Davis Travel Photography 8 (bottom), 24 (top); Mary Evans
7 (both), 9, 24 (bottom); Eye Ubiquitous contents page, 5, 10 (top),
14 (both); Life File 12, 15, 16 (bottom), 17 (top); Wayland Picture Library
title page, 4 (bottom), 13 (top).

Note

The letters 'p.b.u.h' mean 'peace be upon him' and are used whenever the prophet
Muhammad is mentioned in this book.

Contents

What is poultry?

Poultry is the name we give to birds that are kept for their meat, like chickens, turkeys, ducks, geese and guinea fowl. Wild birds which people hunt for their meat, such as grouse and pheasants, are called game. People have kept poultry for thousands of years. It is eaten all over the world by people of many different cultures and religions.

▶ Chicken is a popular food all over the world. Today, we eat ten times the number of chickens that were eaten 50 years ago.

▲ Poultry that has been prepared for cooking. From left to right, they are chicken, poussin (a small, young chicken) and guinea fowl.

4

Poultry has always been a popular food for feasts and celebrations. For many centuries, chickens, turkeys and geese were expensive, and they were fattened for feasts on special occasions. Modern farming methods mean that, in many parts of the world, poultry is produced much more cheaply, and is now eaten all year round for everyday meals. Most poultry today is farmed on big factory farms.

Poultry can be an important part of a balanced diet. Chicken and turkey are the most widely eaten poultry. The meat contains lots of protein, vitamins and minerals but is low in fat, which makes it healthy. Chicken is used for many dishes, from Spanish paella and Chinese chow mein, to roasts and stir frys. It is also a popular fast food, as chicken wings, nuggets, drumsticks and burgers.

▼ Ducks foraging for food in a cottage garden. All over the world, many people still keep poultry in backyards or gardens, as they have done for thousands of years.

5

Poultry long ago

Medieval feasts sometimes included strange dishes. Cokagrys was made by halving a chicken and a pig, and sewing them together.

◀ All chickens, like this cockerel from Sri Lanka, are bred from the wild forest birds that lived thousands of years ago.

Early peoples caught wild birds including ducks and geese in traps, and roasted them over open fires. They may also have dried the meat in the wind or in wood smoke to store it through the winter months. By about 4,000 BC, people had learned how to tame and keep the red jungle fowl, which lived wild in the forests of India and south-east Asia. Gradually, these birds spread to different parts of the world.

The ancient Chinese, Egyptians, Greeks and Romans kept chickens, ducks and geese as well as trapping wild birds. Cockfighting was a popular entertainment. Chickens were also killed as religious sacrifices. The Romans roasted or boiled poultry and served it with spicy sauces.

▶ This Egyptian wall painting, from 1500 BC shows wild birds being hunted for their meat.

◀ A 'chicken man' from 1647.

Medieval poulterers sold both domestic and wild birds caught by fowlers using nets and traps, and cookshops in London sold roasted birds. In the country, most people kept a few hens and sometimes geese and ducks. Hens which were too old for laying eggs were boiled in a pot.

For special occasions and feasts, poultry was fattened up and baked in pastry cases or roasted with rich fruit stuffing and spicy sauces. Cooks used saffron or gold leaf to make a roast look golden, and for the grandest feasts they stuffed several birds one inside another.

Poultry in the past

A Thanksgiving meal of roast turkey. The turkey is traditionally served with cornbread and a cranberry sauce.

Wild turkeys were caught and roasted for the first Thanksgiving feast, held by the Pilgrim Fathers in America in 1621. Turkey is still the central part of the Thanksgiving meal in the USA today.

Guinea fowl originally came from Africa and wild guinea fowl like these can still be found there.

Turkeys first lived wild in Central and North America, where Amerindian peoples used their feathers to decorate headdresses. In the sixteenth century, the Spanish conquistadors brought back turkeys to Europe, where they became known as 'Indian chicken'. Until that time, roast swan and peacock had been the traditional feast dishes of the rich. During the seventeenth and eighteenth centuries, flocks of turkeys were marched to market in London on foot, wearing leather boots or tar on their feet to protect them.

During the seventeenth century, cooks stored poultry by cooking it then potting it in butter, or pickling it in wine or vinegar. Poultry was also boiled in a pot, baked in pastry or roasted with fruit and spices. One of the grandest feast dishes was Yorkshire Christmas pie, made by baking layers of turkey, goose, chicken, partridge and pigeon with butter in pastry.

By Victorian times (1837–1901), roast goose had become the favourite Christmas dish in Britain and other European countries.

Most poultry was kept free range until the 1940s. During the Second World War (1939–45), many people in Europe kept hens in their gardens or backyards while there was a shortage of fresh eggs and meat in the shops. After the war, farmers began breeding some chickens especially for their meat. They kept chickens and other poultry in large barns or in battery cages on egg farms.

▲ A Victorian family choosing their Christmas goose.

Guinea fowl were once called 'turkeys' because they first came to Europe through Turkey. Later, wild birds found in America were also called turkeys because they looked similar to guinea fowl.

9

The food in poultry

Poultry meat is a good source of protein. A 100 g portion of chicken or turkey provides about half the protein an average person needs every day. The protein in poultry is easy to digest so it is especially good for people who are sick or elderly.

A healthy diet is low in fat, especially saturated fats, which are found mainly in meat and dairy foods. Poultry is a healthy food because it is lower in fat than many foods including most other kinds of meat. Eating less fat helps to reduce the cholesterol in our blood. Too much cholesterol can lead to heart disease. A low-fat diet can also help to protect us against other serious diseases.

▲ Skinned fillets of chicken breast. The fat content of poultry is reduced if the skin is removed before cooking, because most of the fat is found just under the skin.

▶ Poultry is a nutritious, low-fat food that contains lots of protein. Protein helps us to grow and repair our bodies in order to stay healthy and active.

Duck and goose contain more fat than chicken and turkey, but all poultry contains polyunsaturated fatty acids, which can help to reduce cholesterol.

Poultry contains B and C vitamins and minerals like iron and zinc, which we need to keep us healthy. Poultry meat can be cooked and served with other healthy foods, such as salads, fresh vegetables and fruit, as part of a balanced diet.

◀ Stir-frying is a healthy, low-fat method of cooking poultry. Grilling and steaming are also low-fat, healthy cooking methods.

100 g of chicken provides:
24. 9 g protein
5.4 g fat
621 kilojoules energy

100 g of duck provides:
25. 3 g protein
10.4 g fat
815 kilojoules energy

Chicken farming

Farmers keep poultry for their meat or eggs. Chickens farmed for meat are called broilers or table chickens. They have been bred to fatten quickly.

Chicks hatch from eggs in incubators which are kept at the temperature of a hen's body. When they are one day old, they are moved to poultry farms. At first they live in brooders, which are sheds kept warm by infra-red lamps.

The farmer then moves them into deep-litter barns, which are large sheds with straw or wood shavings on the floor to collect their droppings. Up to 20,000 birds can live together in a barn. The barn must be kept clean and airy, and have perches where the chickens can roost at night.

▶ Young chicks being fed at a chicken farm in Venezuela. Chicks are fed on special chick feed, which contains protein to help them grow fast.

These young chickens will be kept indoors until they are large enough to be killed for meat. Chickens kept in this way produces cheap meat for people to buy, but the chickens have very little freedom.

Chickens are given water and food which contains cereals, vegetable and animal protein and grit to help them digest it. The food may also contain extra vitamins and minerals, and antibiotics to prevent disease.

Chickens are killed when they are about 42 days old. Poussins, which are small, young chickens, are killed at only 28 days old. The birds are loaded into crates and taken by lorry to a meat-processing plant where they are killed. They are hung by their feet from moving belts and given an electric shock to stun them before their throats are cut by machine blades. The birds are then plucked by machines, ready for preparation and packing for delivery to shops and supermarkets.

Most chickens are processed by machines but, on many farms around the world, plucking is still carried out by hand.

Poultry farming

This duck farm is in a dry, desert area in Egypt. Water was taken from the River Nile to fill the pond.

Turkeys and guinea fowl can be farmed in deep-litter barns. Turkey eggs are hatched in incubators. As one-day old poults, they are moved to brooders where they are kept warm for a few weeks. Then they are kept in barns with the sides open to the air and straw or wood shavings on the floor. One shed can house up to 10,000 birds.

The birds are given water and food which contains protein to help them grow fast, and antibiotics to stop disease. Turkeys are killed when they are between 12 and 26 weeks old.

Guinea fowl are farmed in deep litter barns and killed when they are nine or ten weeks old. Ducks are kept in barns or yards, and killed at seven or eight weeks, when they weigh 1.3–3 kg.

Turkeys on a large poultry farm in Greece.

Many people think that factory farming is cruel. Some farmers keep poultry using a free-range system. Most free-range poultry live in sheds but spend about half of their lives in outdoor runs, where they can scratch about for food. The farmer gives them fresh water and extra food which contains protein. This is a more expensive way to produce poultry, but the birds live a more natural life.

Organic farmers keep poultry in free-range conditions and do not use any chemicals in their farming methods. Organic farming is thought to be better for the environment.

▲ Free-range geese grazing in a frosty field in winter.

Processing poultry

Poultry is sold fresh or frozen or is processed into dishes like soups and canned or chilled ready meals.

At the meat-processing plant, factory workers remove the heads, feet and offal. For freezing, poultry is first chilled in water to stop bacteria growing, then dried, weighed and packed before it is frozen in huge blast freezers. 'Oven ready' poultry may be stuffed, and have fats and flavourings added under the skin.

▲ Fresh poultry, like this chicken, is chilled and packed whole, or cut into portions such as breast fillets, thighs, drumsticks and wings.

Poultry portions can be coated with flaked potato, breadcrumbs or batter and sold chilled or frozen. Meat stripped from the bones is chopped up and mixed with soya protein, then shaped into sticks, rolls, sausages, nuggets or burgers.

◄ Chicken or turkey nuggets like these are coated in batter or breadcrumbs and sold as ready meals or fast food.

Poultry meat can be used to make soups, sandwich spread, pies and pasties. Ready meals include poultry which has been cooked in sauces then canned or chilled, ready to reheat in an oven or microwave. Poultry is also used for fast foods, such as deep-fried chicken wings and nuggets.

Chickens' and ducks' feet may be sent to the Far East, where they are eaten as a delicacy. Poultry offal that humans cannot eat is cooked at very high temperatures to kill all bacteria then used in animal feed and fertilizers.

▲ This man in Cambodia is selling feather dusters, made from dyed poultry feathers. Feathers are also used to stuff pillows, cushions and duvets.

Poultry livers may be sold separately or made into liver paté. Foie gras is a very rich paté from France, made with the livers of geese or ducks. The birds are force-fed with maize to fatten them and enlarge their livers.

► This uncooked goose liver will be used to make foie gras paté.

17

Cooking poultry

There are many ways to cook poultry. It can be roasted, boiled, stewed, grilled, stir-fried, barbecued, steamed or microwaved.

Whole birds are usually roasted. Portions such as breast fillets, are good for grilling, barbecuing, steaming or stir-frying as they keep flavour and moisture. Thighs and drumsticks are good for longer methods of cooking such as stewing and casseroling. Minced poultry meat can be used to make burgers, meat sauces and pies.

Low-fat methods such as grilling, steaming and stir-frying are the healthiest ways of cooking poultry.

▲ A whole roast chicken. The best way to test if a roast bird is thoroughly cooked is to pierce the fattest part of the leg. When it is properly cooked, the juices run clear, not pink or red.

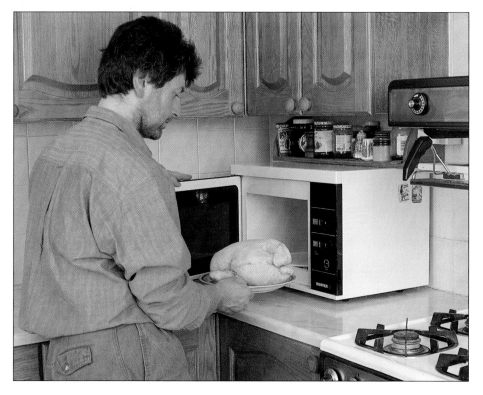

Poultry must be cooked thoroughly, as it can contain the bacteria salmonella and campylobacter, which can cause food poisoning. Microwaving is a good way of ensuring that poultry is cooked right through.

Fresh poultry should be kept in a refrigerator at below 5° C and eaten within two to three days. It is important to keep raw poultry away from cooked foods.

Frozen poultry must be thoroughly defrosted before cooking. Portions will need at least six to eight hours, a whole chicken at least 24 hours, and a larger turkey or goose may need up to three days to defrost.

A duck steaming in a bamboo basket over boiling water. This is a healthy way of cooking and is popular in the East.

Poultry dishes from around the world

Poultry is eaten all over the world by people of many different cultures and religions.

Chicken chow mein is a Chinese dish of chicken, stir-fried with ham, mushrooms, bamboo shoots and Chinese cabbage, flavoured with rice wine and soy sauce and served with noodles.

▲ The French dish coq au vin (chicken in wine) is popular in many countries. It is a casserole of chicken, bacon, onions, mushrooms and herbs in red wine.

The Russian dish of chicken Kiev is made by folding pieces of chicken around a filling of butter, garlic and parsley, then coating them with breadcrumbs and deep-frying them.

Paella is a Spanish rice dish made with chicken, shellfish and vegetables, cooked in a large pan called a paellera.

20

Chicken kishk is an Egyptian dish made with pieces of chicken served with rice and a yoghurt sauce thickened with kishk (a kind of dried cracked wheat).

Indonesian satay consists of pieces of chicken grilled on bamboo sticks and served with a soy sauce dip. Jerked chicken is a Caribbean dish using a mix of hot spices.

Chicken is often used to make soup. Waterzooi is a Belgian soup made by cooking chicken in white wine and stock, then thickening it with egg yolks and cream. Mulligatawny is a hot and spicy chicken soup from India, containing chillies and spices. Cock-a-leekie is a Scottish soup made from chicken boiled with pearl barley, leeks and prunes.

▲ In Africa and the Caribbean, hot spices are added to chicken to make this dish, called jambalaya.

◄ In Britain and other parts of Europe, it is traditional to roast a turkey or goose for Christmas. A Christmas goose like this is often served with roast potatoes, vegetables and bread sauce.

Poultry cooking around the world

In many parts of the world, poultry is roasted for special occasions. The Chinese eat chicken to celebrate birthdays, weddings and festivals.

Cooks chop the roast poultry into pieces, then serve it on a large plate. Most people prefer the dark meat eaten from bones like wings and drumsticks. The white meat is served to children.

▲ Japanese Yakitori bars like this sell mainly chicken snacks, like kebabs of meat, livers, hearts, wings and skin, which are dipped in soy sauce.

▼ Tandoori chicken, an Indian dish of chicken marinaded with yoghurt, chillies and spicesand traditionally cooked in a clay tandoor oven.

Every part of the bird, including the heart, liver and feet are used in special dishes.

Duck is smoked or wind-dried then roasted to make the skin really crispy.

Two duck dishes from Thailand – slices of roast duck served with sauce, and a duck curry.

In African, Caribbean, Indian and Eastern cooking, poultry is often marinaded in spices before cooking, to add colour and flavour.

In the Middle East, the meat from young poultry is often grilled. Older birds are stuffed, then roasted or steamed, or stewed with vegetables, dried fruit, herbs and spices.

In North Africa, chicken is often cooked in a tajine, which is a clay pot with a cone-shaped lid. Dried fruit, almonds, lemons and olives may be added for flavour.

The Aztecs, who lived in Central America until the sixteenth century, kept turkeys. They invented the dish mole poblano de guajolote, which is made with turkey cooked in a sauce containing chilli peppers, nuts and chocolate. The dish is still cooked and is traditionally served at feasts and celebrations.

Poultry customs and beliefs

Cockerels feature in folklore beliefs all over the world. Cockfighting has linked them with bravery and fighting. They have also been seen as representing new life, because they crow at dawn. In classical myth, the cockerel was sacred to the god Apollo.

Cockerels are often seen as messengers, warning of danger or death. They have also been associated with magic and witchcraft, and people once believed that cockerels could scare away ghosts.

▲ On Christian church spires, weather vanes like this are shaped like cockerels as a symbol of protection against evil.

▶ This picture shows Romans carrying some geese in a procession. In 390 BC, the noisy geese had warned the Romans that they were about to be attacked by the Gauls. The Romans carried a golden goose in procession to the Capitoline hill every year to celebrate the event.

The 'cock of Barcelos' is a Portuguese story about a cockerel which was roasted and served to a judge who had just sentenced a pilgrim to be hanged. The cockerel came back to life and told the judge that the pilgrim was innocent. The judge gave the pilgrim his freedom. A similar story is told in parts of Spain, and in one town a live cockerel is kept in the church.

In Japan, cockerels wander freely in temples as they cannot be harmed or killed. In China, white cockerels are believed to protect against evil spirits. The cockerel is also important in Islamic belief as it was the bird seen in the first heaven by Muhammad (p.b.u.h).

◄ A model of the Cock of Barcelos. Painted cockerels like this can be seen all over Portugal.

In Africa, parts of Asia and the Pacific countries, cockerels are seen as messengers from beyond our world. Some tribal peoples still kill cockerels as religious sacrifices, and believe that they can tell the future by examining the dead birds' offal.

Geese appear in nursery rhymes and folk tales, such as 'The goose that laid the golden egg'. This is a Greek story about a man who has a goose that lays golden eggs. The greedy man kills the goose so that he can take all her golden eggs and so loses his magic supply of gold.

25

Poultry recipes for you to try

Lemon chicken

To serve four people you will need:

4 skinless, boneless chicken breast
   fillets
100 g butter, softened
juice of 1 lemon

grated zest of 1 lemon
150 ml soured cream
pinch of salt and pepper
1 tablespoon water

1 Heat the oven to 190° C (375° F, gas mark 5). Put the butter and the lemon zest into a bowl and mix together well.

2 Ask an adult to help you to make three diagonal cuts in each chicken breast, then rub the butter into the cuts.

3 Arrange the chicken pieces in a shallow ovenproof dish.
Sprinkle with the lemon juice, salt and pepper.
Cook in the oven for about 25 minutes,
until the chicken is cooked through.
Lift the chicken into another dish
and keep it warm.

4 Add the water to the cooking
dish, and stir it round, scraping
up any juices. Warm in the oven
for one or two minutes, then stir
in the soured cream, and heat
through in the oven for another
few minutes. When it is hot,
pour over the chicken.

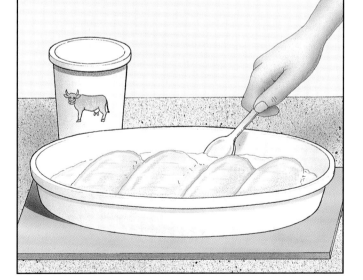

Serve with fresh vegetables or
a salad.

Turkey bolognaise

To serve four people you will need:

450 g raw turkey, minced
1 medium onion, chopped
1 green pepper, chopped
400 g tinned chopped tomatoes
1 garlic clove, crushed
30 ml tomato purée

1 teaspoon chopped herbs
15 ml olive oil
150 ml chicken, turkey or
  vegetable stock
pinch of salt and pepper
300 g dried spaghetti

1 Ask an adult to help you to heat the oil in a pan until hot. Add the garlic and the turkey mince. Stirring all the time, cook until the meat is no longer pink.

2 Add the rest of the ingredients to the pan and stir well. Cover the pan so it is just bubbling and leave to cook for about 15–20 minutes.

3 While the turkey sauce is cooking, ask an adult to help you to heat a pan of water until it is boiling.

4 Add the spaghetti and a pinch of salt. Stir, and bring the water back to the boil, then cover and cook for as long as it tells you on the spaghetti packet (usually about 12–15 minutes).

5 When the spaghetti is cooked, drain it in a colander. Put it into a warmed dish and pour over the turkey sauce.

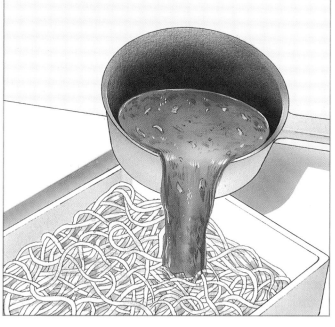

Serve with a salad.

29

Glossary

Amerindians The native peoples of America.

antibiotics Medicines used to destroy bacteria and cure some illnesses.

bacteria Tiny living plants. Some are helpful but others can be harmful.

battery cages Cages in sheds used for keeping chickens, usually for their eggs.

bazaars Markets.

blast freezer Freezers that freeze food with blasts of cold air.

cholesterol A substance found in our bodies and some foods, which can cause heart disease.

classical myth Traditional stories from ancient Greece or Rome.

conquistadors Spanish explorers who conquered America in the fifteenth and sixteenth centuries.

defrosted A frozen item that has thawed, so that no ice is left.

delicacy Food that is eaten as a special treat.

factory farms Farms where food is produced as quickly and cheaply as possible.

fillets Pieces of meat that have had the bones removed.

food poisoning An illness caused by eating food that contains certain types of bacteria.

folklore Stories, myths and legends of a certain people or area.

fowlers Wild bird catchers.

free range A system of keeping farm animals or poultry which allows them to spend some of their lives outdoors.

incubators Machines that keep eggs warm, ready for hatching.

infra-red Special rays which give light and warmth.

kebabs Grilled meat or vegetables, usually threaded on to sticks and sometimes marinaded before being cooked.

kilojoules A measurement of the energy in food.

marinaded Soaked in a liquid before cooking. The liquid usually contains wine, vinegar, oil, herbs or spices.

medieval From the period of the fifth to the fifteenth century.

minerals Substances found in some foods, which we need to keep us healthy.

nutritious Containing goodness.

offal Heart, liver and other body organs.

organic A system of farming without using chemicals.

Pilgrim Fathers The first settlers in America.

plucked With feathers removed.

30

polyunsaturated fatty acids A kind of fat found in some foods, which can lower cholesterol in the blood.

poulterers People who keep shops selling poultry.

poults Young turkeys or pheasants.

predators Animals or birds which eat other animals or birds.

processed Prepared for storage or cooking.

sacrifices Things that are killed or given up for religious or other reasons.

saffron The orange part of a crocus flower, which is used for colouring and flavouring food.

saturated fat A kind of fat found in some foods, which can cause heart disease.

spires Tall pointed towers on top of churches or other buildings.

stir-frying A way of cooking food quickly by stirring it in hot oil in a wok (Chinese frying pan) or a frying pan.

Thanksgiving A feast to give thanks for the harvest, first eaten by the first settlers in America in 1621.

tribal Peoples who live in groups under a leader and share history and beliefs.

vitamins Substances found in some foods, which we need to keep us healthy.

weathervanes Objects that are marked with the points of the compass and spin in the wind to show wind direction.

Books to read

Farming Now: Chickens by Joy Palmer (Hodder & Stoughton, 1989)

Let's Visit a Poultry Farm by Sarah Doughty & Diana Bentley (Wayland, 1989)

For further information about poultry, contact:

The British Chicken Information Service
Educational Project Resources
Bury House
126–128 Cromwell Road
London SW7 4ET

British Turkey Information Service
Glen House
125 Old Brompton Road
London SW7 3RP

Index